D1226790

THE UNTOLD STORIES
OF OUR NAMES
A TO Z

STORIES & ILLUSTRATIONS BY LIO YEUNG

• • •

THIS BOOK BELONGS TO

_____

• • •

To my daughter Lilka,

Although Shakespeare may have been right about
a rose smelling just as sweet by any other name,
may this book make you smile about yours,
remind you of where you came from,
and lead you back home – wherever the future takes you.

Love you always.

Aaron is a giant.

Meaning
Mountain of strength

Origin
Hebrew

Pronunciation
AIR-en

Adam is made of dust.

Meaning
First man

Origin
Hebrew, English

Pronunciation
A-dəm

Agnes is innocent.

Meaning
Holy

Origin
Greek, Latin

Pronunciation
AG-nəs

Alan likes to rock 'n roll.

Meaning
Rock

Origin
Celtic, Gaelic

Pronunciation
AL-in

Albert is popular.

Meaning
Famous, bright, noble

Origin
English, German

Pronunciation
AL-bərt

Alexander is superhuman.

Meaning
Like God

Origin
Greek, Latin

Pronunciation
al-ik-ZAN-dur

Amanda is full of love.

Meaning
Worthy of love, lovable

Origin
English, Latin

Pronunciation
uh-MAN-dah

Amelie
multi-tasks.

Meaning
Hardworking

Origin
French, German

Pronunciation
AH-mə-lee

Amy is
a serial dater.

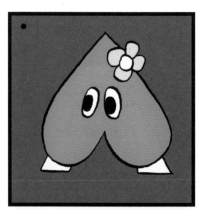

Meaning
Beloved

Origin
English, French

Pronunciation
AY-mee

Anastasia is not a ghost.

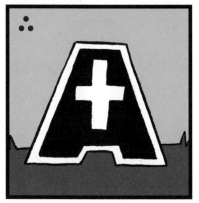

Meaning
Resurrection

Origin
Greek, Russian, Slavic

Pronunciation
ah-nah-stah-SEE-yah /
a-nə-STAY-zhə

Andrew is fearless.

Meaning
Manly, brave

Origin
English, Greek, Scottish

Pronunciation
AN-droo

Angela uses air mail.

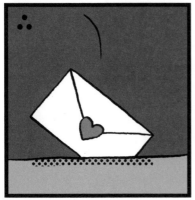 

Meaning
Messenger of God, angel

Origin
English, Greek, Italian, Latin

Pronunciation
AN-jəl-ə / AHN-he-lah

Angus is full of ideas.

Meaning
Unique strength, wisdom

Origin
Celtic, Gaelic, Irish, Scottish

Pronunciation
ANG-gəs

Anna is generous.

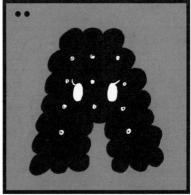

Meaning
Grace, graciousness

Origin
Hebrew, Latin

Pronunciation
AN-a / AHN-a

Anthony
is special.

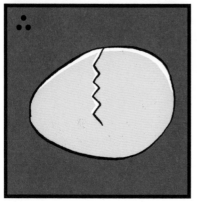

Meaning
Priceless

Origin
English, Latin

Pronunciation
AN-tha-nee

Ashley lives in the woods.

Meaning
Ash tree meadow

Origin
English, Gaelic, Irish

Pronunciation
ASH-lee

Bella is gorgeous.

Meaning
Beautiful

Origin
Italian

Pronunciation
BEL-ah

Benedict is a lucky charm.

Meaning
Blessed

Origin
English, Latin

Pronunciation
BEN-ə-dikt

Benjamin is from the south.

Meaning
Son of the south

Origin
English, Hebrew

Pronunciation
BEHN-je-min

Bianca likes cleaning.

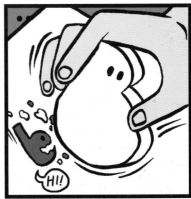

Meaning
White, fair, pure

Origin
Italian

Pronunciation
bee-AHN-ka / BYAHN-kah

Billy is tough.

Meaning
Strong protector

Origin
English, German

Pronunciation
BILL-ee

Bobby parties too hard.

Meaning
Shiny, famed, bright

Origin
English

Pronunciation
BAH-bee

Bonnie is lovely.

Meaning
Fair of face, pretty

Origin
Scottish

Pronunciation
BOHN-ee

Brian likes to yodel.

Meaning
High, noble

Origin
Celtic, Gaelic, Irish

Pronunciation
BRIE-ən

Bruce is into calligraphy.

Meaning
Willow woods, thick brush

Origin
Scottish

Pronunciation
BROOS

Burt is made of bricks.

Meaning
Fortified enclosure / town

Origin
English

Pronunciation
BUR-t

Candy is a sweetheart.

Meaning
Sweet, shiny, bright

Origin
English

Pronunciation
KAN-dee

Carol is in disguise.

Meaning
Manly, strong

Origin
English

Pronunciation
KER-əl

Celine lives in the sky.

Meaning
Heavenly, sky

Origin
French, Latin

Pronunciation
SE-LEEN

Chanel is a pipe.

This is not a pipe

This is a painting

This is a Chanel

She is a pipe

Meaning
Canal, water pipe

Origin
French

Pronunciation
sha-NEL

Charles is hairy.

Meaning
Manly

Origin
English, French, German

Pronunciation
CHAHRLZ

Charlotte has a parachute.

Meaning
Free woman

Origin
English, French, German

Pronunciation
SHAHR-lət

Cherry is fruity.

Meaning
The fruit, dear one, darling

Origin
English

Pronunciation
CHER-ee

Chloe is an early bloomer.

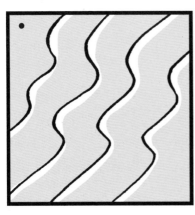

Meaning
Young green shoot, vibrant

Origin
English, French

Pronunciation
KHLOH-ee

Christopher has a conscience.

Meaning
Christ-bearer

Origin
English, Greek

Pronunciation
KRIS-tə-fər

Claire wears a lot of bling.

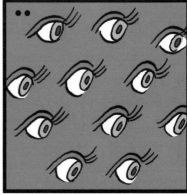

Meaning
Bright, clear

Origin
French, Latin

Pronunciation
KLAYR

Coco is juicy.

Meaning
Coconut, help

Origin
Spanish, French

Pronunciation
KO-ko

Cody is made of feathers.

Meaning
Cushion, pillow, helpful person, prosperity

Origin
English, Gaelic

Pronunciation
KO-dee

Cole dislikes barbecues.

Meaning
Coal black

Origin
English

Pronunciation
KOHL

Cyrus is into astronomy.

Meaning
Sun, lord

Origin
Persian, Greek

Pronunciation
SYE-rəs

Daisy cannot make decisions.

Meaning
The flower, day's eye

Origin
English

Pronunciation
DAY-zee

Dana is from Denmark.

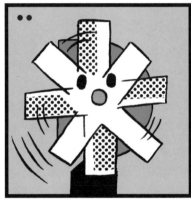

Meaning
From Denmark, brave, generous, wise

Origin
Celtic, Irish, Nordic

Pronunciation
DAY-na / DAH-na

Daniel is mischievous.

Meaning
God is my judge

Origin
English, Hebrew

Pronunciation
DAN-yul

David likes kisses.

Meaning
Beloved, darling

Origin
English, Hebrew

Pronunciation
DAY-vid

Dax goes with the flow.

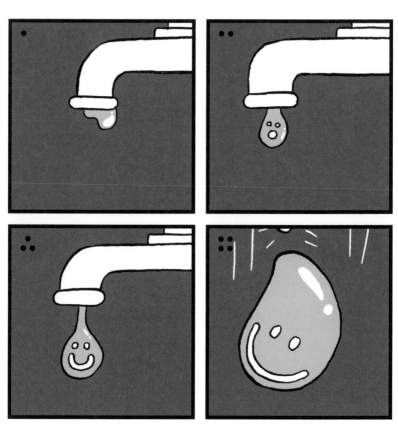

Meaning
Water, badger

Origin
French, German

Pronunciation
DAKS

Diana is a goddess.

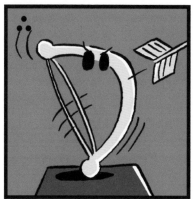

Meaning
Divine, sky

Origin
English, Greek, Latin

Pronunciation
dye-ANN-uh

Donald is a chief.

Meaning
Ruler of the world

Origin
Celtic, Scottish

Pronunciation
DAHN-əld

Dylan is afraid of sharks.

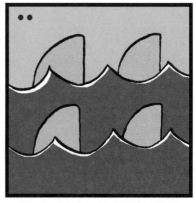

Meaning
The sea

Origin
Celtic, Welsh

Pronunciation
DILL-in

Edmund is a security specialist.

Meaning
Protector of riches, blessed

Origin
English

Pronunciation
ED-mund

Edward is a gym buff.

Meaning
Guardian of wealth / happiness

Origin
English

Pronunciation
EHD-werd

Elizabeth makes promises.

Meaning
Pledge to God

Origin
English, Hebrew

Pronunciation
ə-LIZ-ə-bəth

Ellen uses a lot of electricity.

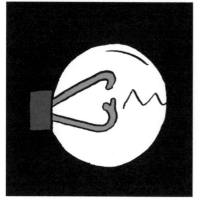

Meaning
Ray of light, sunbeam

Origin
English

Pronunciation
EL-ən

Elsa is easily contented.

Meaning
God is my oath, God's promise

Origin
English, German

Pronunciation
EL-sa

Elvin likes elves.

Meaning
Elf's friend

Origin
English

Pronunciation
EL-vin

Emily is competitive.

Meaning
Eager, rival, industrious

Origin
English, Latin

Pronunciation
EM-ə-lee

Emma wants to be popular.

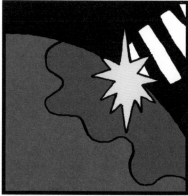

Meaning
Universal, whole, complete

Origin
English, French

Pronunciation
EM-ə

Eric likes to measure things.

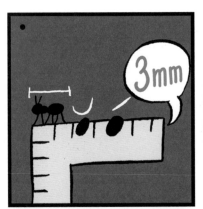

Meaning
Eternal ruler

Origin
Nordic

Pronunciation
AIR-eck

Ethan is ageless.

Meaning
Long-lived, firm

Origin
English, Hebrew

Pronunciation
EE-thin

Eve is a shape-shifter.

Meaning
Mother of life

Origin
English, Hebrew

Pronunciation
EEV

Evelyn is nutty.

Meaning
Hazelnut, a living being, desired, wished for

Origin
English, German

Pronunciation
EV-ə-lin

Fanny likes French things.

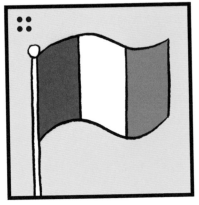

Meaning
From France, free

Origin
French, Latin

Pronunciation
FAN-ee

Faxon has long locks.

Meaning
Long-haired, thick-haired

Origin
German

Pronunciation
FAKS-en

Felix hits jackpots.

Meaning
Fortunate, happy

Origin
Latin

Pronunciation
FEE-liks

Ferris is cool under pressure.

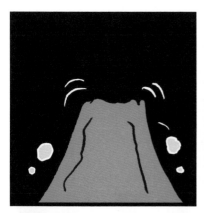 

Meaning
Rock

Origin
English, Gaelic, Scottish, Irish

Pronunciation
FEH-ris

Filia is friendly.

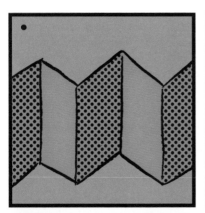

Meaning
Friendship, amity

Origin
Greek

Pronunciation
FEE-lee-ah

Fitch is furry.

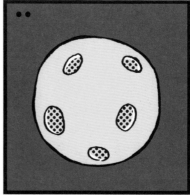

Meaning
Ermine, ferret-like animal

Origin
English, French

Pronunciation
f-IH-ch

Francis loves the forest.

Meaning
Tree, French man

Origin
English, French

Pronunciation
FRAN-sis

Frank is trustworthy.

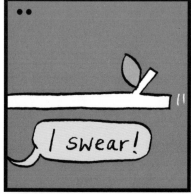

Meaning
Honest, free landholder,
French man

Origin
English

Pronunciation
FRANK

Galvin likes to fly.

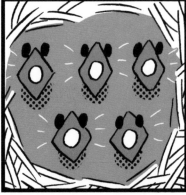

Meaning
Sparrow, glowing, white

Origin
Irish, Gaelic

Pronunciation
GAEL-VihN

Gemma is precious.

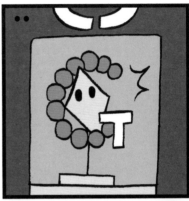

Meaning
Jewel, gem, precious stone

Origin
Italian, Latin

Pronunciation
JEM-ə

Genesis likes new beginnings.

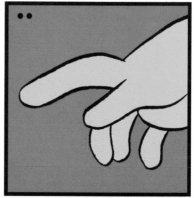

Meaning
Beginning, origin

Origin
English, French, Greek, Latin

Pronunciation
JEN-ə-sis

George is full of life.

Meaning
Farmer, earth worker

Origin
English, French, Greek, Latin

Pronunciation
JOHRJ

Gertrude is sharp.

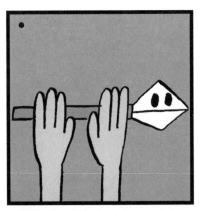

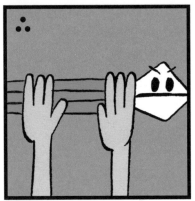

Meaning
Spear of strength

Origin
Dutch, German

Pronunciation
GUR-trood

Gloria loves to win.

Meaning
Glory

Origin
English, Latin

Pronunciation
GLAWR-ee-ə

Hadil makes happy sounds.

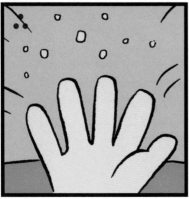 

Meaning
Cooing of a pigeon

Origin
Arabic

Pronunciation
HA-DIL

Hana is optimistic.

Meaning
Flower, grace, hope, happiness

Origin
Jewish, French, Kurdish, Persian, Japanese

Pronunciation
HA-NA

Harper likes to tell stories.

Meaning
Minstrel

Origin
English

Pronunciation
HAHR-pər

Hazel loves squirrels.

Meaning
Hazel tree, creativity, knowledge

Origin
English

Pronunciation
HAY-zel

Heather is good-natured.

Meaning
Flowering plant

Origin
English, Scottish

Pronunciation
HEH-thər

Henry is sturdy.

Meaning
Ruler of the home

Origin
English, French

Pronunciation
HEN-ree

Hilary likes to smile.

Meaning
Cheerful

Origin
English, Latin

Pronunciation
HIL-ə-ree

Hugo is smart.

Meaning
Mind, heart, spirit

Origin
French, German

Pronunciation
HYOO-go

Ian has a good heart.

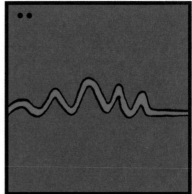

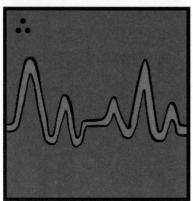

Meaning
God is gracious

Origin
Gaelic, Scottish

Pronunciation
EE-in

Iggi is one of a kind.

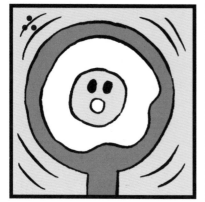

Meaning
Only son

Origin
African

Pronunciation
IGGI

Iris is colourful.

Meaning
Rainbow

Origin
Greek

Pronunciation
EYE-riss

Isabelle makes pinky promises.

Meaning
God is my oath, devoted to God, God's promise

Origin
French

Pronunciation
iz-ah-BEHL

Isaac laughs a lot.

Meaning
He laughs

Origin
Hebrew

Pronunciation
I-zik

Ivy is a decorator.

Meaning
Climber, symbol of friendship

Origin
English

Pronunciation
EYE-vee

James is a good substitute.

Meaning
At the heel, the supplanter

Origin
English

Pronunciation
JAYMZ

Jayden likes approval.

Meaning
God has heard

Origin
American

Pronunciation
JAY-din

Jenny likes water.

Meaning
White, smooth

Origin
English

Pronunciation
JEHN-nee

Jeremy is an escape artist.

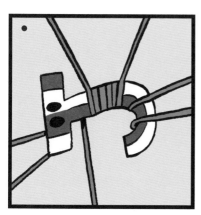

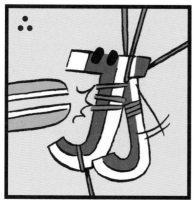

Meaning
Appointed by God,
Yahweh has established,
the Lord exalts

Origin
English, Hebrew

Pronunciation
JEHR-ə-mee

Jerry is not afraid of monsters.

Meaning
May Jehovah exalt

Origin
Hebrew, English

Pronunciation
JAIR-ee

Jessica is a secret agent.

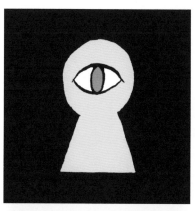

Meaning
Foresight, clairvoyance

Origin
English, Hebrew

Pronunciation
JEH-sə-kah

Jonah is a destroyer.

Meaning
He who oppresses

Origin
Hebrew

Pronunciation
JO-nah

Jonathan
makes wishes.

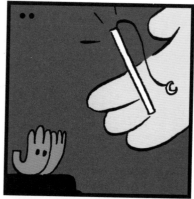

Meaning
God has given, friendship, loyalty

Origin
English, Hebrew

Pronunciation
JAHN-ə-thən

Joseph likes being lifted up.

Meaning
May Jehovah add / give increase

Origin
English, Hebrew

Pronunciation
JO-sehf

Joyce is taking over the world.

Meaning
Lord, joyous, vivacious

Origin
Celtic, English

Pronunciation
JOIS

Julia has soft hair.

Meaning
Soft-haired, youthful

Origin
Latin

Pronunciation
JEW-lee-ah

Juno is a queen.

Meaning
Queen of heaven, young, lamb

Origin
Latin, Irish

Pronunciation
JU-NO

Karen is transparent.

Meaning
Pure one, innocent

Origin
Nordic

Pronunciation
KARE-in

Karl is a farmer.

Meaning
Free man, tiller of the soil

Origin
German

Pronunciation
KAHRL

Keith is exemplary.

Meaning
From the place of battle, wood, forest

Origin
Celtic, Gaelic, Scottish

Pronunciation
KEETH

Kelvin sheds tears.

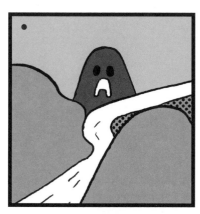

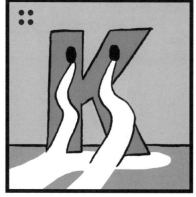

Meaning
Narrow rivers

Origin
Celtic, Gaelic, Scottish

Pronunciation
KEHL-vin

Kingston is royal.

Meaning
King's village

Origin
English

Pronunciation
KING-stən

Krystal likes to sparkle.

Meaning
Crystal

Origin
American, Greek

Pronunciation
KRIS-təl

Leia needs sunshine.

Meaning
Heavenly flowers

Origin
Hebrew, Greek

Pronunciation
LEE-ah / LAY-ah

Leonardo is brave.

Meaning
Brave lion

Origin
Italian, Spanish

Pronunciation
lee-oh-NAHR-doh

Liam is a helmet.

Meaning
Helmet of will, protector

Origin
Gaelic, Irish

Pronunciation
LEE-əm

Lila sleeps all day.

Meaning
Night, dark beauty

Origin
Hebrew, Arabic

Pronunciation
LIE-la

Lilka is delicate.

Meaning
Lily, warrior maiden

Origin
Polish

Pronunciation
LIL-ka

Lloyd likes soot.

Meaning
Grey

Origin
Welsh

Pronunciation
LOYD

Logan lives in a tiny home.

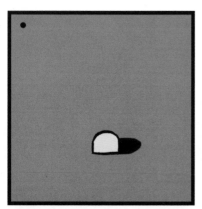

Meaning
Little hollow

Origin
Gaelic

Pronunciation
LOH-gən

Lucas likes celebrations.

Meaning
Bringer of light

Origin
English, Greek, Latin

Pronunciation
LOO-kas

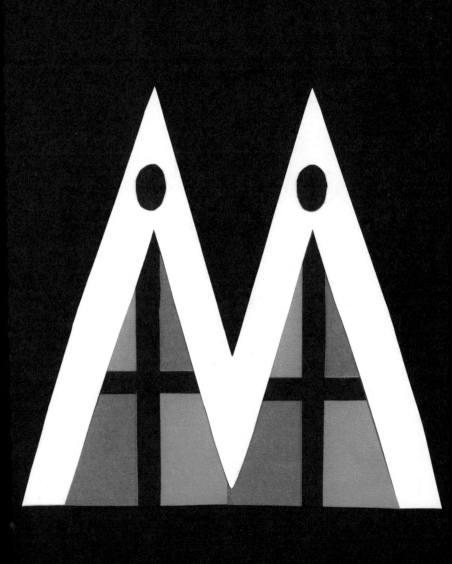

Maggie loves dressing up.

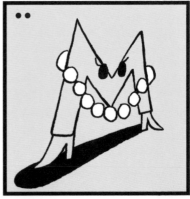

Meaning
Pearl

Origin
English

Pronunciation
MA-gee

Manolo is never alone.

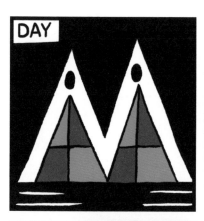

Meaning
God is with us

Origin
Spanish, Greek

Pronunciation
mah-NOH-loh

Mark hates wars.

Meaning
God of war, male, virile, steed, horse

Origin
Celtic, English, Irish

Pronunciation
MAHRK

Mary is a rebel.

Meaning
Bitterness

Origin
Hebrew

Pronunciation
MER-ee / MAIR-ee

Matthew is a gift.

Meaning
Gift of God

Origin
English, Hebrew

Pronunciation
MATH-yoo

Max loves pushing limits.

Meaning
Maximum

Origin
Latin

Pronunciation
MAHKS

Melissa likes honey.

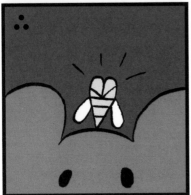 

Meaning
Honey bee

Origin
English, Greek

Pronunciation
me-LIS-ah

Mia
loves herself.

ME

MY VEST

ME & VEST

ME MYSELF & I
WEARING MY VEST

Meaning
Mine, beloved, wished for

Origin
Dutch, German, Italian,
Latin, Nordic

Pronunciation
MEE-ah

Morgan lives by the sea.

Meaning
Sea circle, phantom queen, magnanimous

Origin
Celtic, Gaelic, Irish

Pronunciation
MORE-gahn

Morris
is tanned.

Meaning
Dark-skinned, swarthy

Origin
Latin

Pronunciation
MOR-us

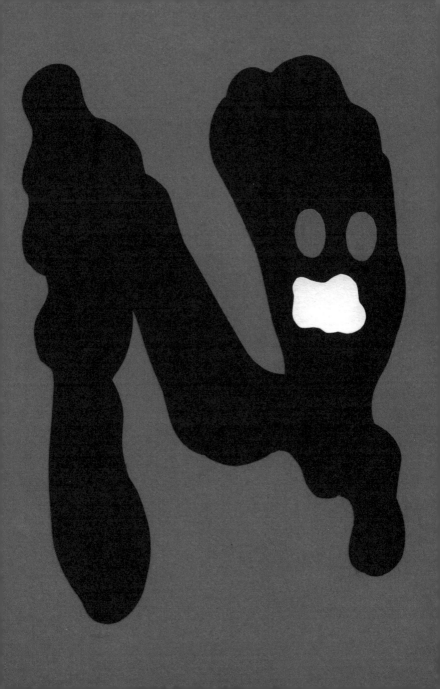

Nata is a good swimmer.

Meaning
Hope, speaker, swimmer

Origin
Polish, Native American

Pronunciation
NA-TA

Natalie likes cake.

Meaning
Christmas day, birthday

Origin
English, French, Latin

Pronunciation
NAD-ah-lee

Natasha loves Christmas.

Meaning
Born at Christmas

Origin
Russian

Pronunciation
nə-TASH-ə

Nathan is an artist.

Meaning
He has given

Origin
English, Hebrew

Pronunciation
NAY-thən

Nicholas always wins.

Meaning
People of victory

Origin
English, Greek

Pronunciation
NIK-ə-lis

Nigel is easily spooked.

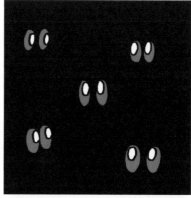

Meaning
Black, champion, passionate

Origin
English, Latin

Pronunciation
NEYE-jul

Noah wants world peace.

Meaning
Peace-maker, rest, comfort

Origin
English, Hebrew

Pronunciation
NO-ə

Nolan is a high achiever.

Meaning
Champion, chariot-fighter

Origin
Gaelic, Irish

Pronunciation
NO-lin

Oda grows plants.

Meaning
Rice paddy, long voyage, wealth

Origin
Japanese, German

Pronunciation
OH-də

Oliver likes peace.

Meaning
Olive tree, peaceful

Origin
French, English

Pronunciation
AHL-ə-vər

Omega likes endings.

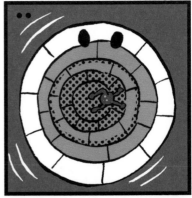

Meaning
The end

Origin
Greek

Pronunciation
o-MAY-gə

Oscar plays with deer.

Meaning
Friend of deer

Origin
Celtic, Gaelic, Irish

Pronunciation
AHS-ker / OH-skar

Otto makes a lot of money.

Meaning	Origin	Pronunciation
Wealth, prosperity, fortune	German	AH-toe / AW-toe

Owen is fancy.

Meaning
Well-born, youthful

Origin
Celtic, Greek, Welsh

Pronunciation
OH-wen

Pandora likes surprises.

Meaning
All gifts

Origin
Greek

Pronunciation
pan-DOHR-ə

Parker obeys the rules.

Meaning
Park-keeper, gamekeeper

Origin
English

Pronunciation
PAHR-ker

Patrick is noble.

PATRICK I

PATRICK II

PATRICK III

PATRICK JR

Meaning
Nobly born

Origin
Celtic, Gaelic, Irish

Pronunciation
PAT-rik

Paul is small.

Meaning
Small, humble

Origin
English, Latin

Pronunciation
PAWL

Peter is a weapon.

Meaning
Stone, rock

Origin
English, Greek

Pronunciation
PEE-ter

Phoebe twinkles at night.

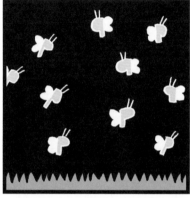

Meaning
Bright, the radiant one

Origin
Greek, Latin

Pronunciation
FEE-bee

Phoenix is immortal.

Meaning
Crimson, rising bird, symbol of renewal, rebirth

Origin
Greek, Latin

Pronunciation
FEE-niks

Prudence is careful.

Meaning
Cautious, good judgement

Origin
English, French

Pronunciation
PRU-dents

Quacy is nosy.

Meaning
Of the moonlight

Origin
Scottish

Pronunciation
KWAY-see

Queenie is regal.

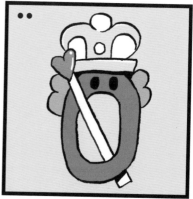

Meaning
Royal lady, ruler

Origin
British

Pronunciation
KWEEN-ie

Quentin likes high-fives.

Meaning	Origin	Pronunciation
Fifth	French, Latin	KWEN-tin

Quiana is smooth.

Meaning
Silky

Origin
American

Pronunciation
kee-AHN-ah

Quillan is nimble.

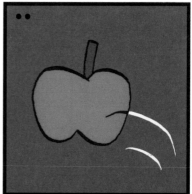

Meaning
Little sword, cub

Origin
Gaelic, Irish

Pronunciation
kwee-lən

Quinn is fair.

Meaning
Counsel, wise

Origin
Gaelic, Irish

Pronunciation
KWIN

Rachel likes to dream.

Meaning
Ewe, lamb

Origin
Hebrew

Pronunciation
RAY-chul

Raymond loves animals.

Meaning
Wise protector

Origin
French, German

Pronunciation
RAY-mund

Rebecca has many friends.

Meaning
Join / tie

Origin
English, Hebrew

Pronunciation
rə-BEHK-ah

Richard leads an army.

Meaning
Powerful, strong, brave

Origin
English, French

Pronunciation
RICH-ərd

Rihanna is a witch.

Meaning
Witch of goodness, great queen

Origin
African-American, Celtic, Welsh

Pronunciation
ree-AN-ə

Ringo is delicious.

Meaning
Apple

Origin
Japanese

Pronunciation
RING-go

Ronald is muscular.

Meaning
Having God's power, wise ruler

Origin
Nordic

Pronunciation
RAHN-awld / RON-uld

Roy is well-groomed.

Meaning
Red

Origin
English, Scottish

Pronunciation
ROY

Ruby is a gem.

Meaning
Red gemstone

Origin
English, Latin

Pronunciation
RUE-bee

Ryan wears a tiny crown.

Meaning
Little king

Origin
Celtic, Gaelic

Pronunciation
RYE-ən

Sally has a curfew.

Meaning
Princess

Origin
English

Pronunciation
SAL-ee

Samantha is rowdy.

Meaning
God has heard, listener

Origin
American

Pronunciation
sa-MAN-tha

Scarlett hurts easily.

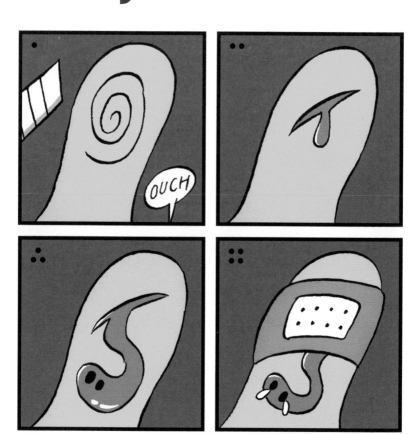

Meaning
The colour red, rich cloth

Origin
English, French

Pronunciation
SKAR-let

Simon loves music.

Meaning
Listen / hear

Origin
English, Hebrew

Pronunciation
SY-mon

Sophia is brainy.

Meaning
Wisdom

Origin
English, Greek

Pronunciation
so-FEE-uh

Stella glows in the dark.

Meaning
Star

Origin
Latin

Pronunciation
STEL-lah

Taylor is skilful.

Meaning
Tailor, to cut

Origin
English

Pronunciation
TAY-ler

Thomas always thinks twice.

Meaning
Twin

Origin
English, Greek

Pronunciation
TAH-məs

Tiffany likes to pray.

Meaning
God appears

Origin
English, Greek

Pronunciation
TIF-ə-nee

Timothy
sings well.

Meaning
Honour God

Origin
English, Greek, Latin

Pronunciation
TI-mə-thee

Titania is a titan.

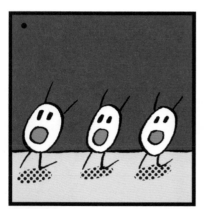

Meaning
Giant, the great one

Origin
Greek

Pronunciation
tit-TAHN-ya

Toby is a blessing.

Meaning
God is good

Origin
English

Pronunciation
TOE-bee

Tony likes praise.

Meaning
Praiseworthy

Origin
English, Latin

Pronunciation
TOE-nee

Travis is undecisive.

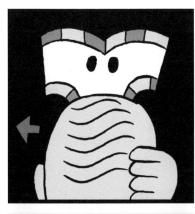 

 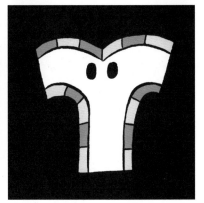

Meaning
Crossroads

Origin
English, French

Pronunciation
TRA-vis

Tristan wears an armour.

Meaning
Knight

Origin
Celtic

Pronunciation
TRIS-tin

Tyler
makes tiles.

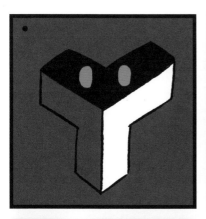

Meaning
Tile-maker

Origin
English

Pronunciation
TIE-ler

Una likes being the first.

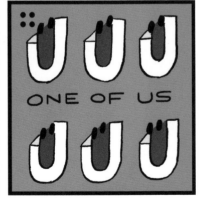

Meaning
One

Origin
Latin

Pronunciation
OO-nah

Ursula is fierce.

Meaning
Little she-bear

Origin
Latin

Pronunciation
UR-sə-la

Usha likes daylight.

Meaning
Dawn

Origin
Hindi, Sanskrit

Pronunciation
oo-shah

Uta cannot sing.

Meaning
Song

Origin
Japanese

Pronunciation
oo-ta

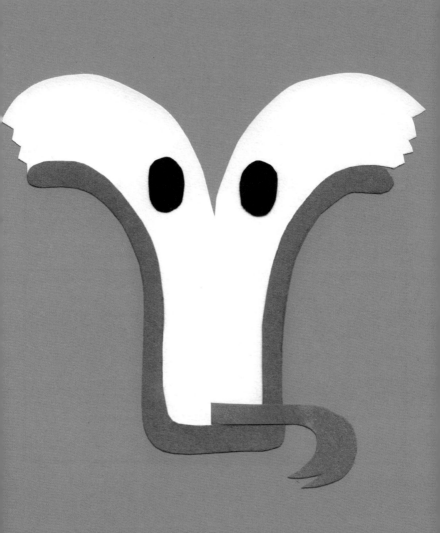

Vanessa has a sweet tooth.

Meaning
Butterfly, mystic

Origin
English

Pronunciation
Va-NESS-ah

Veda is
a bookworm.

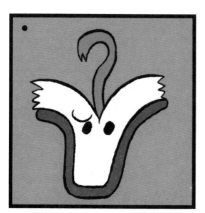

Meaning
Knowledge

Origin
Sanskrit

Pronunciation
VEH-da

Veronica is into politics.

Meaning
True image, she who brings victory

Origin
Latin

Pronunciation
və-RAHN-i-kə

Victor
never loses.

Meaning
Victor, conqueror, winner

Origin
Latin, Spanish

Pronunciation
VIK-ter

Violet is not violent.

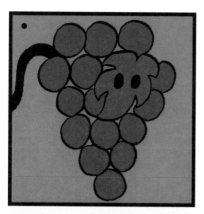

Meaning
The colour purple, flowering plant

Origin
English, French

Pronunciation
VIE-ə-let

Viva is a daredevil.

Meaning
Alive

Origin
Latin

Pronunciation
VIVA

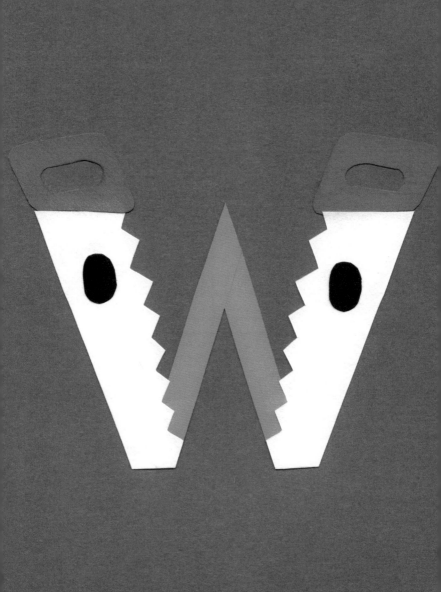

Wesley is dramatic.

Meaning
Western wood clearing, meadow

Origin
English

Pronunciation
WEHS-lee

Whitney is always by herself.

Meaning
White island

Origin
English

Pronunciation
WIT-nee

William is hardy.

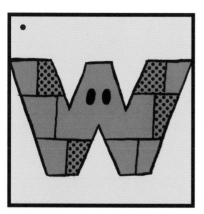

Meaning
Valiant protector

Origin
English, French, German

Pronunciation
WIL-yem / WIL-ee-im

Wright likes to fix things.

Meaning
Shaper of wood

Origin
English

Pronunciation
RA-it

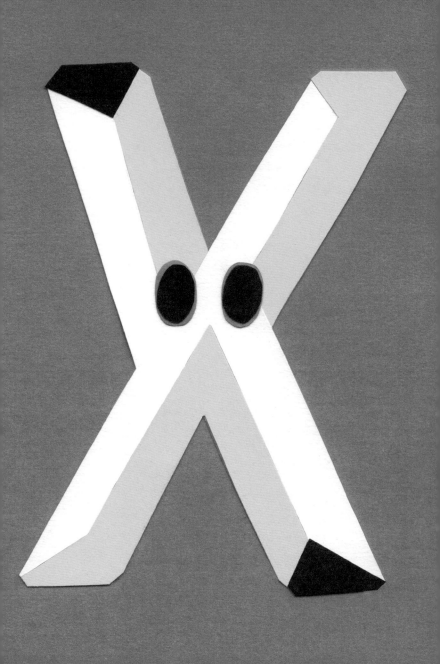

Xanthe is flashy.

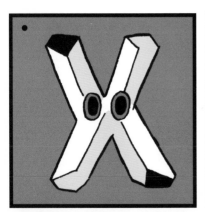

Meaning
Gold

Origin
Greek

Pronunciation
ZAN-thee

Xavier buys a lot of houses.

Meaning
New house

Origin
Spanish

Pronunciation
ZAY-vyer / ehk-SAY-vyer

Xenia likes meeting people.

Meaning
Welcoming, hospitable

Origin
Greek

Pronunciation
ZE-niya

Xylander is an environmentalist.

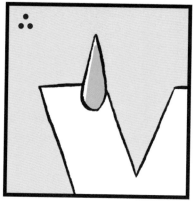

Meaning
Man of the forest

Origin
Greek

Pronunciation
ZAI-lǝhn-der

Yaron thinks he can sing.

Meaning
To shout / sing

Origin
Hebrew

Pronunciation
YA-ren

Yasmin smells nice.

Meaning
Jasmine

Origin
Arabic, English

Pronunciation
YAZ-min / yaz-MEEN

Yogi is flexible.

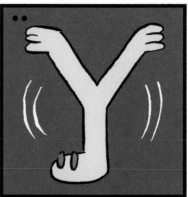

Meaning
Of the yoga practice

Origin
Hindu

Pronunciation
YO-GI

Yoko is bubbly.

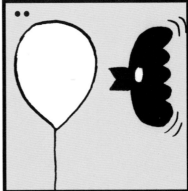

Meaning
Sunshine child

Origin
Japanese

Pronunciation
YOH-ko

Yuki is gentle.

Meaning
Snow, happiness

Origin
Japanese

Pronunciation
YOO-kee

Yvette has poor aim.

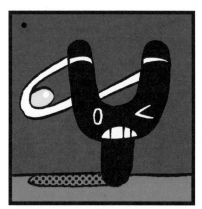

Meaning
Archer, yew

Origin
French

Pronunciation
e-VET

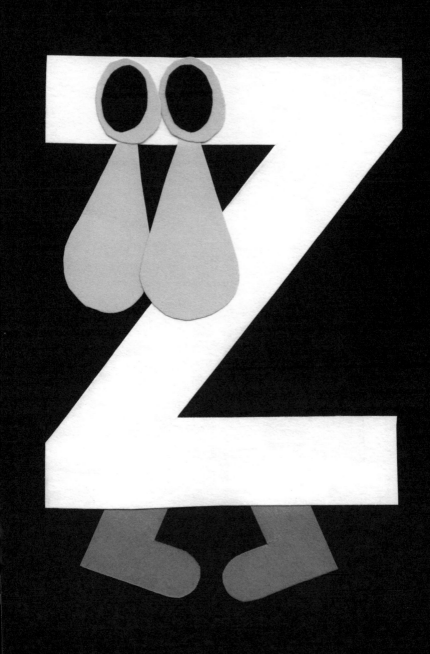

Zareh cries at everything.

Meaning
Tears

Origin
Armenian

Pronunciation
ZA-reh

Zelda is hard to beat.

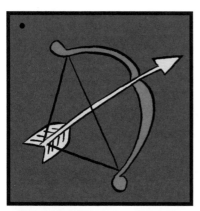

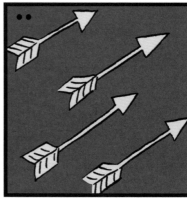

Meaning
Dark battle, companion

Origin
German

Pronunciation
ZEHL-də

Zendaya has a bad back.

Meaning
To give thanks

Origin
African

Pronunciation
zehn-DAY-ə

Zetta has a lucky number.

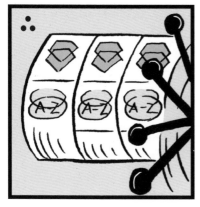

Meaning
Seven

Origin
Latin

Pronunciation
ZET-tə

Zita can find anything.

Meaning
Seeker

Origin
Greek, Italian, Hungarian

Pronunciation
ZEE-ta

Zoe lives for adventures.

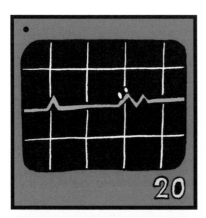
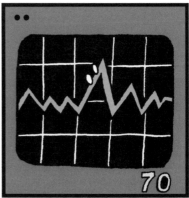
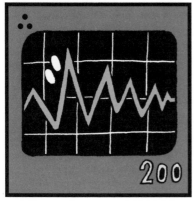

Meaning	Origin	Pronunciation
Life	Greek	ZOH-ee / ZOH

Name Library

A

Aaliyah is the feminine version of the name Aali or Ali. It means 'to ascend', 'lofty', or 'sublime' in the Arabic language.

Aaron is a name that most likely originated from the Bible. It means 'mountain of strength' in the Hebrew language.

Abel is mostly associated with the notable Biblical character. In Hebrew, the name means 'breath', or 'breathing spirit'.

Abigail is a Hebrew name in the Bible that means 'my father's delight' or 'father rejoiced'. It was borne by King David's wife.

Abraham does not have a literal meaning in the Hebrew language. In the Bible, it was given to 'a father of a multitude'.

Adalyn is a combination of the names Ada and Lynn, and means 'noble'. It could also be a variant of Adeline or Adelina.

Adam was the Biblical name of the very first man God created out of dust. In Hebrew, it refers to 'man', 'earth', or 'ground'.

Addison means 'Adam's child' in Old English. It used to be a surname before becoming a popular given name in modern times.

Adrian is a form of the Latin name Adrianus or Hadrianus. It was likely inspired by the Venetic word meaning 'sea' or 'water'.

Agnes was derived from the Greek word 'hagnos' which means 'pure'. It reached peak popularity during the Middle Ages.

Aidan in the Gaelic language means 'like a fire', and is thought to be the anglicised form of the Irish name Aodhan.

Alaina is a variant of Elaine, a French name that originated from the Greek Helene – which means 'light', 'torch', or 'bright'.

Alan was derived from the Celtic word 'alp, ail' which means 'rock'. It can also be found in the modern Irish word 'ailín'.

Albert has Germanic roots, specifically the words 'adal' which means 'noble', and 'berht' which means 'bright' or 'famous'.

Alejandro is a Spanish variant of the Greek Alexandros, derived from the words that mean 'to ward off' or 'defend' and 'man'.

Alexa is the short form of Alexandra, which originates form the Greek language. It is said to mean 'protector of humanity'.

Alexander was derived from the Latin Alexandros, originally a Greek name. It is usually associated with might and power.

Alice is said to have originated from the Old French language, and means 'noble' or 'graceful'.

Alina has a few origins. In German, it is a dimunitive of Adele which means 'noble', while in Slavic, it means 'bright'.

Allison is an alternate spelling of Alison, which was derived from the name Alice. In Old French, it means 'noble' or 'graceful'.

Alyssa could refer to the Alyssum flower, or a variant of Alicia – which is the modern Latin version of the name Alice.

Amanda is said to have originated from the Latin word 'amanda', which means 'worthy of love' or 'lovable'.

Amelie blends the Latin Emilia and the Latinised German Amalia, which originated from the word 'amal' which means 'work'.

Amy originated from the Old French word 'amee' or the Latin word 'amata' in the Middle Ages, to refer to one loved by many.

Anabel was influenced by the name Anna, as a variant of the name Amabel. In Latin, Amabel means 'adorable'.

Anastasia is the feminine form of the ancient Greek name Anastasius, which is associated with 'ressurection'.

Andrea originated from the Greek language and means 'daring'. It is said to be the feminine form of the name Andrew.

Andrew is the anglicised form of the Greek Andreas, which was derived from the word 'andreios' which means 'masculine'.

Angela is the feminine form of Angelus which means 'angel', and was derived from the word 'angelos' which means 'messenger'.

Angus is the anglicised form of the Gaelic Aonghas, which is composed of the Celtic elements meaning 'one' and 'choice'.

Anna is thought to be a variant of the name Hannah, which means 'gracious' or 'favoured' in the Hebrew language.

Anthony is the anglicised form of the old Roman family name Antonius, which refers to someone praiseworthy.

Aria refers to air or the word for an expressive melody performed by a singer. It could also be from the Hebrew word meaning 'lioness'.

Ariana is a variant of the name Ariadne, which originates from the Greek language and means 'the holiest one'.

Ariel was popular amongst Christians in the olden days as it means 'God's lion' in the Hebrew language.

Asher originated from the Bible, and was given to Jacob's eighth son. In the Hebrew language, it means 'fortunate', or 'blessed'.

Ashley was originally a surname that came from the Old English elements that mean 'ash' and 'clearing' or 'meadow'.

Ashton originated from Old English and means 'town of ash trees'. It was derived from the name of a place and used as a surname.

Athena was a famous figure in Greek folklore as the goddess of wisdom, warfare, strength and justice.

Aubrey originated from the Germanic languages, and is said to refer to the 'ruler of elves'.

Audrey is a name that has its roots in the Old English language, and means 'of noble strength'.

Aurora is said to be from the Latin language and means 'sunrise'. It could also refer to the name of the natural light display.

Austin originated from the Latin Augustine, which means 'dignity' or 'venerable'. It was developed in the Middle Ages.

Autumn originated from the Latin language, and is a name that is typically associated with the season of fall.

Ava is likely to have come from the Latin word 'avi' which means 'bird' or 'bird-like'. It could be a derivative of Eve which means 'life' or 'lively'.

Avril is said to be a variation of the name April, which originated from the Latin language. Some sources say that it was derived from an expression that means 'open'.

B

Bailey originated from the Middle English language and was most likely derived from the profession of a governor, or bailiff.

Bain or **Bains** is a name that originated from Scotland and was derived from the Gaelic word meaning 'white' or 'fair'.

Barak is a name that is found in the Bible, and originated from the Hebrew language. It is said to mean 'lightning' or 'fire bolt'.

Bassa or **Bassem** is said to have originated from the Arabic language and roughly means 'one who smiles'.

Bautista is the Spanish variant of the French Baptiste, which was derived from the Greek word which means to 'dip in water'.

Beatrix originated from the Latin language, and means 'voyager'. It was borne by several saints in the Christian world and royalty.

Behrouz or **Behrus** originated from the Persian language, and means 'having good luck' or literally, 'good day'.

Bella is commonly associated with the Italian word which means 'beautiful', or the Latin word 'bellus' which means 'pretty, fair and charming'.

Benedict is the anglicised form of the Latin word 'benedictus' which means 'blessed'. It was borne by the founder of the Benedictine Order.

Benjamin originated from the Bible, and was most likely a translation of 'son of the south' in the Hebrew language.

Bennett is a name that sources say was derived from the English name Benedict, which means 'blessed' in the Latin language.

Bentley is the name of several places in England. It originated from the Old English words meaning 'bent grass' and 'a clearing'.

Bertie is the pet form of the name Albert or Alberta, which originated from the Germanic languages and means 'wise' or 'graceful'.

Bianca is an Italian name that originated from the Latin word 'blancus', which means 'white' or 'pure'.

Billy is a shortened form of the Germanic name Wilhelm, which is composed of 'wil' ('will' or 'desire') and 'helm' ('helmet' or 'protection').

Bjorn originated from the Old Norse language, and means 'bear'. It used to be common in its native Scandinavia.

Blake could have originated from the Old English words 'blac' which means dark, or 'blaac' which means 'fair' or 'pale'.

Bleu is a French word that refers to the colour blue. It is a unique but uncommon given name in its native country.

Bo is most commonly used in Chinese-speaking countries and means 'wave-like'. It could also have been derived from Old Norse language.

Bobby is a shortened form of Robert, which originated from the old Germanic name that means 'fame', 'glory', or 'bright and shining'.

Bonnie is a name that means 'pretty' in Scottish, and was probably derived from the French word 'bonne' which means 'good'.

Bradley was originally used as a surname in Old English, derived from the name of a place that means 'broad clearing'.

Bran is a name that originated from the Old English language, and means 'raven', or 'a hillside covered with broom'.

Braxton is a name that originated from the Old English language, and was inspired by the name of a place, Browston.

Bree originated from the Irish language and means 'hill' or 'higher power'. It could also be the shortened form of Brina and Breanna.

Brian is an Irish name that most likely comes from an old Celtic-Gaelic word 'brigh' which means 'noble' or 'high'.

Brianna is thought to be the feminine version of the Irish name Brian, and most likely means 'the noble one'.

Brielle is the short form of the name Gabrielle, which originated from the Hebrew language and means 'God's bravest woman'.

Brody was originally used as a surname in the Irish community. It is rooted in the Gaelic language and means 'waterway'.

Brooke originated from the Old English language and means 'from a stream'. It used to function as a surname.

Brooklyn means 'from the land of the broken' in Dutch, but is more popular in English-speaking countries as a given name.

Bruce was originally a Scottish surname of Norman origins, most likely referring to the town of Brix in France.

Bryce originated from the French language, and means 'speckled'. It was derived from the name Byrchan.

Burt is thought to be the shortened form of an old English town called Burton, which means 'fortified enclosure'.

C

Caesar is a variant for the Latin name Cesar, which means 'to be hairy' or 'head of hair'. Its origins are uncertain.

Cajsa is the Swedish incarnation of the popular Greek and English name Katherine, which means 'chaste' or 'pure'.

Caleb originated from the Hebrew language, and can be found in the Bible. It is said to mean 'to be faithful'.

Calista is from the Greek language and means 'woman of most beauty'. It could also be the feminine form of Callistus.

Calvin is a name that has multiple origins. In French, it is a form of the name Chauve, which means 'little bald one'.

Camden used to be an Old English surname that comes from the words 'camp' and 'denu', which mean 'enclosure' and 'valley'.

Camelia is associated with the flower of the Camille group, which is in turn associated with moon, water, and perfection.

Candy was derived from the Cushitic word meaning 'queen mother'. In modern times, it is associated with sweets and confectionary.

Carmelo is the Spanish/Italian variant of the name Carmel, which is originally from the Hebrew language and means 'garden of god'.

Carol is a feminine form of the name Charles that was derived from the old Germanic word 'karl' which means 'free man'.

Carter is an English name that was most likely derived from the occupation of 'the one who uses a cart'.

Carville or **Carvil** used to be an English surname that most probably means 'house on the rock' or 'stone house'.

Casey originated from the Gaelic language and means 'alert' or 'watchful'. It was derived from an old Irish surname.

Cassius was derived from the Latin word 'cassus' which means 'empty'. It has been borne by several saints over time.

Catalina is the Spanish form of Katherine, which means 'chaste' or 'pure' in the Greek language.

Cecilia originated from the Latin language, and means 'blinded'. It has been popular since the late 19th century.

Celine is the French variation of the name Celeste, which means 'heavenly' in Latin. It could also describe the heavens, sky or outer space.

Chakrii or **Jakrii**, as it is sometimes spelt, originated from the Thai language and means 'king' or 'royalty'.

Chanel was originally derived from the French word 'chanel', which itself is from the Latin word 'canalis' which means 'water pipe'.

Charles is said to be the French and English version of Karl or Carl, derived from the Germanic word 'karl' which means 'free man'.

Charlotte is the feminine form of the name Charles that originated from France. The latter is said to mean 'free man'.

Cheng originated from the Chinese language, and could mean 'completed', 'succeeded' or 'sincere' depending on how it is written.

Cherry simply refers to the sweet fruit in modern times. It could also be from the Latin word 'charitas' which means 'generous love'.

Chikere comes from the African languages and means 'created by God'. It is uncommon in English-speaking countries.

Chloe is a name that originated from the Greek language, and can also be found in the Bible. It means 'little green sprout'.

Christopher is the anglicised form of the Greek name Khristophoros, which essentially means 'bearer of Christ'.

Claire is a French name that was derived from the Latin word 'clārus', which means 'bright, clear, and distinct' or 'illustrious and shining'.

Claude is a variant of Claudia, the feminine version of Claudius. It originated from the Latin language and means 'feeble'.

Coco is a name that most probably began as a French nickname for Nicolette, which means 'people's victory'.

Cody originated from an old Gaelic nickname that was given to a helpful person. It could also allude to the 'prosperity' in German.

Cole originated in the Middle Ages from the English nickname Cola, which means 'having a weather-beaten complexion'.

Collin was derived from the name Nicholas, which originated from the Greek language and means 'people's triumph'.

Conn originated from the Gaelic language, and was originally a surname. It could also have been derived from Connor, and means 'leader'.

Constance is a name that originated from the Latin language, and is the feminine form of Constant. It means 'steady' or 'permanent'.

Cora is thought to be a variant of the name Corinna, which originated in the Greek language and means 'maiden'.

Cyrus is the anglicised form of the Greek name Kyros which was believed to have been associated with a lord.

D

Daewon is a Korean name with different meanings, depending on how it is written. The more popular variation means 'gracious God'.

Dagwood is a name that originated from the English language, and literally translates to 'shining forest' or 'bright wood'.

Daichi originated from the Japanese language, and is made up of the words that mean 'impressive' and 'son'.

Daisy is a name that was derived from the flower and Old English word that means 'day's eye'.

Dakota is said to have originated from the Lakota Sioux language and means 'friendly companion'.

Dana is most likely related to Daniel, a Hebrew name which means 'God is my judge'. It could also refer to someone from Denmark.

Daniel is borne from the Old Testament in the Bible and means 'God is my judge' in the Hebrew language.

David is a name that is heavily associated with Christianity and means 'beloved man' in the Hebrew language.

Dax could be an early English surname derived from 'badger' in German, or the name of a small town in France, which means 'water'.

Delilah is a name that can be found in the Bible. It originated from the Hebrew language and means 'delicate woman'.

Dev is a given name that originated from the Sanskrit language, and is mainly used in India. It is also popular as a surname.

Diana is found in Roman mythology and refers to the goddess of the hunt, the moon, forests and childbirth – or Artemis in Greek.

Diego is a Spanish name that originated from the Latin language, and was derived from the word 'didacus' which means 'doctrine'.

Dominique is a French name that originated from the Latin language, and means 'Lord's child'. It is the feminine form of Dominic.

Donald is the anglicised version of the Scottish name Domhnall, which contains the Celtic words meaning 'world', and 'rule'.

Dorothea is said to be the feminine version of the Greek name Dorotheos, which means 'gift of God'.

Dyani or **Dayanni** is a name of Native American origins, and means 'deer' or 'resembling a deer'.

Dylan is connected to an old Welsh noun which refers to the sea. In Celtic mythology, it is associated with the Son of the Wave.

E

Ebele originated from the African language and is said to mean 'compassion' and 'kindness'. It has been popular in Nigeria for many years.

Edelmar is a name of Germanic origins, and is said to be derived from the words 'edel' and 'mar' meaning 'noble'.

Edmund is a popular name that is composed of the Germanic elements 'ead' ('rich' or 'blessed') and 'mund' ('protector').

Edric is an Old English name, which was derived from the words 'ead' and 'ric' – meaning 'wealthy' and 'ruler' respectively.

Edward is of Anglo-Saxon origins and is composed of the Germanic elements 'ead' or 'prosperity', and 'weard' or 'guard'.

Ekin is a name that originated from the Turkish language, and means 'harvest' or 'crop'.

Eleanor originated from the Greek language, and means 'sympathy' or 'compassion'. It could also mean 'one who heals' in Latin.

Electra is a modern name that is rooted in Greek origins and means 'shining' or 'radiant'.

Eli originated from the Hebrew language, and is a name that means 'high', 'ascended', or 'my God'.

Eliana is a given name with Hebrew, Latin, Greek, and Arabic roots. It denotes 'my Lord responded' in Hebrew.

Elin is a name with multiple Slavic origins, and generally means 'torch of light'. In Welsh, it also refers to 'the most beautiful woman'.

Elizabeth has been around since the Middle Ages in various forms. It is Biblical and said to mean 'pledge to God'.

Ellen was developed as an English form of Helen, which most likely originated from 'helios' – the Greek word for 'sun'.

Elmas is a name that has Turkish and Persian origins. It is said to mean 'like a diamond'.

Elsa is said to be the shortened form of the name Elisabeth, which is the French, German and Dutch form of Elizabeth.

Elva is the anglicised version of the name Alibhe, which originated from the Gaelic language and means 'fair' or 'white'.

Elvin is a name that was most probably derived from an old English name that contained elements which mean 'elf' and 'friend'.

Emery has Germanic origins and means 'brave' or 'powerful'. It was derived from Emmerich, which originated from 'labour' and 'ruler'.

Emily is the English version of the Latin name Aemilia, which came from the Latin word 'aemulus' meaning 'striving to excel'.

Emma is a shortened, evolved form of ancient names like Ermintrude and Irmengarde, and means 'universal' in German.

Emmett is a name that sources say was derived from the name Emma, which has Germanic origins and means 'universal'.

Enoch can be found in the Bible. It originated from the Hebrew name Chanokh, which means 'dedicated' or 'faithful'.

Erdem is a name that originated from the Turkish language, and means 'virtuous'. It is a popular given name.

Eric is related to the Old Norse name Eirik, which was derived from the Germanic words 'ei' ('ever' or 'always') and 'rikr' ('ruler').

Erika is the Czech version of the name Erica, which originates from the Old Norse language and means 'ruling forever'.

Erol may have originated from the Turkish language, and refers to a 'man with courage'.

Ethan is a popular Biblical name that originated from the Hebrew language, and means 'long-lasting' or 'enduring'.

Evan was derived from the name Iefan, a Welsh variant of the name John. The latter is Hebrew for 'God is merciful'.

Evangeline is a name that originated from the Greek language, and is made up of the words that mean 'good' and 'news'.

Eve is a Biblical name that actually originated from the Hebrew word 'havva', which means 'living' or 'animal'.

Evelyn is either a diminutive form of Eve, or derived from the old French name Aveline and refers to a hazelnut in German.

Everly originated from the English language, and was the name of a place. It means 'from a wild boar meadow'.

Evita is the shortened version of the name Eva, which originated from the Hebrew language and means 'living' or 'breathing'.

Ezra is a popular name that was derived from the Hebrew word 'ezer', which means 'help'. The name itself means 'God is help'.

F

Faith is a name that originated from the Latin language, and carries the same meaning as the word itself, which is 'trusting' or 'believing'.

Fanny is said to be a diminutive form of French names like Frances, Francoise or Stephanie.

Farah is a popular name in the culture from which it came. It has Arabic roots and means 'happy' or 'joyful'.

Faxon is thought to have originated from the Old German word which means 'long-haired'.

Felix has joyous connotations as it comes from the Latin word for 'happy'. It also denotes fortune, good luck, and success.

Ferris is anglicised version of the Old Gaelic name, O' Fearghusa – with the elements 'fear' or 'a man' and 'gus' or 'vigour'.

Filia is a name that is thought to be a form of Ophelia, which sources say originated from Greek and means 'help' or 'support'. As the tragic heroine in William Shakespeare's play Hamlet, it is also one of the most analysed female names in all of English literature.

Fiona is the feminine version of the name Fionn. It originated from the Gaelic language and means 'fair woman'.

Fitch originated from an ancestor who hunted or kept fitches, which are ferret-like creatures.

Flint originated from Old English language. It was used as a nickname for a person who was 'as hard as flint'.

Francis gained popularity in the 14th century and referred to a man from France, or a tree. It was borne by a notable saint.

Frank is the shortened form of Francis, which is a name that refers to a Frenchman.

G

Gabriel originated from the Hebrew language and means 'God's bravest man'. It has different spellings all over the world.

Gail is the short form of the name Abigail, which originated from the Hebrew language. It means 'my father's delight'.

Gaines is an English name that was derived from the Old French word 'engaingne' and the Latin word that means 'ingenuity'.

Galvin is thought to mean 'sparrow' or 'brilliantly white' in Irish. It also stems from the Old French word 'galer' or 'to enjoy oneself'.

Gazsi came from Gaspar, which is a Hungarian version of the name Jasper. In Persian, it means 'king of the treasure'.

Gemma or **Gema** started as an Italian nickname which dates back to the Middle Ages, and probably refers to the jewellery.

Genesis is a Biblical name that was ultimately derived from the Greek word 'genesis' which means 'origin' or 'creation'.

Genevieve is a popular English name, but its roots lie in the Germanic language and means 'leader of the tribe'.

George is said to have originated from the Greek word 'georgos' which means 'farmer'. It has always been a popular name.

Gerardo is the Spanish/Italian version of the name Gerard, which is rooted in the Germanic language and means 'strong like a spear'.

Gertrude is a classic name with Germanic origins, composing of words that mean 'spear' and 'strength'.

Gianna was derived from the name Giovanna. Its masculine form, Giovanni, is from the Hebrew John, which means 'God is merciful'.

Gil is the short form of the name Gilbert, based on the Old Germanic words 'gisil' and 'berht'– meaning 'noble youth' and 'bright'.

Gillian is said to have come from the Latin language and means 'daughter of Jupiter'. It could also have been derived from Julia.

Gloria is a name that comes from the Latin word meaning 'glory'. It essentially refers to prestige, respect, and admiration.

Grace embodies the meaning of the word in the English language, which is 'elegant' and 'graceful'. It is popular in the Christian world.

Graham is actually a name that is based on a place called Grantham, which means 'grand homestead' in the Old English language.

Grant was actually derived from the Old French word 'graunt' and the Latin word 'grandis', which mean 'tall' or 'great'.

H

Hadil is actually a variant of the name Hadeel, which is largely used in the Arabic world. It refers to 'the cooing of a dove or pigeon'.

Hahn has many origins, with meanings that differ according to how it is written. In the Germanic language, it means 'rooster'.

Hakim is a name that originated from Arabic culture. Literally translated, it means 'wise' and was one of Prophet Mohamed's names.

Haloke is an unusual name with Native American origins and means 'salmon'.

Hana is most commonly associated with the Persian and Japanese word that means 'flower'.

Hang is a name with uncertain origins and its meaning differs according to where it is used. In Vietnamese, it means 'moon'.

Harmony is a name that originated from the Greek language and generally refers to the art of using chords in music.

Harper started off as an English surname referring to a harp player, which originated from the Old English word 'hearpere'.

Haruki is a Japanese name that has different meanings depending on how it is written. It is usually associated with spring and wood.

Hayley was derived from an Old English surname that means 'meadow of hay'. It could also be the Old Norse word meaning 'heroine'.

Hazel originated from the English word signifying wisdom as the tree itself has nut-like fruits that could signify nuggets of knowledge.

Heather is a name based on the English word defining the flowering plant indigenous to the moorlands of Europe.

Hedwig originated from the Germanic language and was given to several notable saints. It means 'fighting a battle'.

Heidi was derived from Adelheid, which is the German form of Adelaide and means 'graceful' and 'noble'.

Helle is the Danish variant of Helga, an Old Norse name that means 'divine woman'. It is also the feminine form of Helge.

Henry comes from the Old German name Heimerich, which was derived from the Germanic elements 'haim' ('home') and 'ric' ('rule').

Hilary is said to have originated from the Latin word 'hilaris' which means 'of good cheer'.

Hugh originated from the Germanic word 'hug' meaning 'heart, mind, and spirit'. In medieval France, it referred to an intelligent person.

I

Ian is the Scottish-Gaelic version of John and was ultimately derived from the Hebrew Yochanan which means 'God is gracious'.

Ida originated from the Germanic language, and refers to a 'hardworking woman'. It is mostly popular in Scandinavian countries.

Iggi is a name that has been used in the African region for centuries. It is thought to mean 'the only son'.

Ilaria is the Italian version of Hillary, which was derived from the Latin word that means 'cheerful' and 'merry'.

Imogen comes from the Gaelic language and means 'young maiden'. Some sources say that it was actually created by Shakespeare.

Ingfred originated from Scandinavia, and is said to have been derived from the surname 'Ing' and the word meaning 'peace'.

Iris personifies the rainbow or the messenger between gods (i.e. the link between gods and mortals) in Greek mythology.

Irvin is the shortened version of the name Irving, which originated from the Scottish language and means 'water of green'.

Isabelle is the modern French form of Isabel, a name that originated as Elisabeth and means 'God's promise'.

Isla is said to have origins in the Gaelic language. It is the feminine form of Islay, and means 'from the Islay island'.

Isaac is one of the oldest and most significant Biblical names, and means 'he will laugh' in the Hebrew language.

Iver is a variant name of Ivar, which originated from the Old Norse language and means 'fighter with bow'.

Ivy is a name that comes from the English word associated with the evergreen clinging, climbing, or ground-creeping vine.

Izumi is a Japanese name that can bear different meanings, depending on how it is written. It typically associated with 'spring'.

J

Jacques is a French variant of the name Jacob, which was derived from the Hebrew name 'Yaakov' and means 'following after'.

Jade is a popular gemstone that became a modern given name. It originated from the Spanish language.

Jagger is a modern given name that is said to have been derived from the Germanic word 'jeger' which means 'to chase' or 'hunt'.

Jai or **Jay** is an Indian name with Sanskrit origins, and means 'victorious'.

Jamal is a name that is popular in the Arabic-speaking world. It was derived from the word 'jamal' which means 'beauty'.

James was derived from the ancient Hebrew name Yaakov, which came from the word 'akev' and means 'at the heel'.

Jana is said to be the variant of Jane, which originated from the Hebrew language and means 'God is merciful'.

Jareth is a variation of the name Jared or Jarrod. It is popular in the English-speaking world, and means 'descendant'.

Jason was featured in Greek mythology as the Thessalian hero who led the Argonauts. The name means 'a person who heals'.

Jasper originated from the Persian culture and means 'king of the treasure'.

Javier is the Spanish variant of the name Xavier, which was derived from the Basque words 'etche' and 'berria' – meaning 'house' and 'new'.

Jayden is a variant of the Biblical name of Hebrew origin, Jadon, which means 'God has heard'.

Jayla is a modern English name that originated from the name Jay, which was a surname. It usually refers to a jaybird.

Jeana is a variant of Gina, which is the shortened form of Regina. Regina comes from the Latin language, and means 'queen'.

Jed was derived from Jedidiah or Jedediah, which are in the Bible. It has Hebrew origins, and means 'friend of God'.

Jedi may have been popularised by the Star Wars franchise, but actually has Arabic origins. It is said to mean 'the hand'.

Jenny comes from the Welsh name Gwenhwyfar or Guinevere, which was derived from 'gwen' and 'hwyfar' to mean 'the fair one'.

Jeong is a name that can be spelt differently, but is said to have originated from Korea and means 'silent' or 'chaste'.

Jeremy is the anglicised form of Jeremiah, which in turn was derived from the Hebrew Yirmeyah which means 'appointed by God'.

Jerry is a name that is most commonly thought of as a short form of Gerald, which means 'ruling spear'.

Jessica is inspired by a Biblical character called Iscah, who was Abraham's niece. The name likely means 'God sees'.

Jetta was derived from the name Henrietta, which originated from the Germanic language and means 'ruler of the house'.

Jocelyn has roots in a Germanic tribe called the Gauts. It originally means 'German tribal person'.

Johanna was derived from the names Joanna or Joan. Joan is the feminine version of John and means 'God is merciful'.

Jolie is a name that originated from the French language, and translates to 'lovely girl'.

Jonah is a Biblical character that is famous for having been swallowed by a whale. In Hebrew, the name means 'destroyer' or 'dove'.

Jonas is a variant of the Biblical name Jonah. It is said to have originated from the Hebrew language and means 'dove'.

Jonathan is a Biblical name that originated in the Hebrew language. It is seen as a symbol of loyalty and friendship.

Joseph is the anglicised form of the Hebrew name Yosef which translates to '(God) shall add (another son)'.

Jovani is said to be a derivative of Jovan, the Slavic equivalent of the popular English name John which means 'God is merciful'.

Joyce was a derivative form of the ancient Breton name Iodoc, which means 'lord'. Its Latinised form became Jodocus.

Julia was derived from the Latin word 'Iovilios' which means 'pertaining to or descended from Jove'.

Julian was a popular name in Roman times. It originated from the Latin language, and means 'wearing a soft beard'.

Juno is a name that means 'young' in Latin. It was given to the protectress of women and marriage in Roman mythology.

K

Kai is a name with many origins, but is commonly associated with the Hawaiian language and means 'from the sea'.

Kaiser is the German version of the name Caesar, which itself is a variation of the name Cesar which means 'to be hairy'.

Kala is the Hawaiian variant of Sarah, which originated from the Hebrew language and means 'princess' or 'lady-like'.

Kaleb is a modern version of the name Caleb, which is a Biblical name with Hebrew origins and means 'whole-hearted'.

Kalil or **Khaleel** is a name that originated from the Arabic language and translates to 'close friend'.

Kanye may have been popularised by the rap singer, but sources say that it has Hawaiian origins and means 'free'.

Karen is said to be the Danish equivalent of Katherine, which was adopted from the French name Catherine and means 'pure'.

Karl is the German form of Carl or Charles, which is from the same medieval roots as the Old English word that means 'common man'.

Kavita has been a popular name in the Indian community for years. It originated from Sanskrit and means 'poetic'.

Kayla is a modern form of Katherine, a name that originated from the Greek language and means 'chaste' or 'pure'.

Keane is a variant form of Kean, which was derived from Cian – the Celtic word that means 'ancient one'.

Keith originated from the Gaelic word 'ceiteach' which means 'forest'. It could also have been derived from the Old Welsh word for 'wood'.

Kelvin originated in the 20th century, and is taken from a river in Scotland which flows southwest from the central hills.

Kendall was derived from an Old English surname with Germanic origins, and means 'coming from the Kent river valley'.

Kendrick either came from the Welsh language and means 'supreme champion', or from the Old English language and means 'family ruler'.

Kiana is a modern variant of Qiana, which was originally the name of silky nylon fibre that was introduced in the 1970s.

Killian or **Cillian** is originated from the Gaelic language. It is said to mean 'church man'.

Kingston started off as a name of a place, and became a surname with Anglo-Saxon roots. It literally translates into 'king's town'.

Kini is thought to be the Hawaiian variant of the popular English name Jane, and means 'abundance'.

Kinsley is the modern variant of the name Kingsley, which originated from Old English and means 'king's meadow'.

Kir is a Russian form of Cyrus, which is an ancient Persian name. It was derived from the word 'khuru' which means 'throne'.

Kong can have many meanings, depending on how it is written in Chinese. It is most commonly associated with the sky.

Krystal is a name that the English borrowed from the word 'krystallos', which means 'ice' in Greek and signifies a precious gemstone.

Kylie most likely originated from the Gaelic language and means 'living near a narrow channel'.

Lana is the shortened version of the name Alana, which originated from the Germanic language and means 'valuable' or 'precious'.

Lance originated from the Germanic language, and was derived from the name Lanza or Lant, which means 'land' or 'territory'.

Lauren originated from the Latin language. It is said to be the feminine version of Laurence and means 'laurel tree'.

Leah is a Biblical name with Hebrew origins. It has been popular since the Protestant Reformation and means 'delicate woman'.

Leia is a Biblical name that refers to a heavenly flower in Hebrew language. It symbolises a fruitful marriage in Jewish culture.

Leilani refers to the lei, a famous necklace of flowers. In the Hawaiian language, the name is said to mean 'heavenly woman'.

Lenka was derived from the popular English name Helen, which originated from the Greek language and means 'torch of light'.

Leonardo is an Italian/Spanish name derived from the German words 'leon' or 'lion', and 'hard' or 'brave, strong, and hardy'.

Levi is a name with Biblical origins. It comes from the Hebrew langage and means 'connected'.

Lewis is a variant of Louis, which originated from the Germanic language. It was derived from Ludwig, meaning 'well-known fighter'.

Lexi originated from the Greek language and is said to be the feminine form of Alexander, meaning 'protector of humanity'.

Liam is the Irish version of William, which was ultimately derived from the Old Germanic name Willahelm and means 'helmet' or 'protection'.

Lila is a simplified version of the name Leila, which originated from the Arabic language. It has come to mean 'dark beauty'.

Lilka is a name of uncertain origins. However, most sources believe that it was derived from Liliana, which simply means 'lily'.

Lincoln was derived from a place in England, and is made up of the Welsh words that mean 'lake' and 'colony'.

Lindell is a variant of the name Linde, which has Germanic origins. It was derived from the name Lind, which means 'lime'.

Linus originated from the Greek name Linos, which was derived from the Greek word 'lineos' meaning 'flaxen'.

Lloyd was borrowed from the Welsh word 'llwyd', which means 'grey'. It was first used during the Middle Ages.

Logan is a Gaelic surname that contains the word 'log' ('hollow') and the '-an' diminutive – thus meaning 'little hollow'.

Lois originated from the Greek language, and is featured in the Bible as the grandmother of Timothy. It means 'the best'.

Loki is a notable figure in Norse mythology as a trickster god. It was a nickname for anyone considered a cheat.

Lorcan is an uncommon name that was derived from the Gaelic word 'lorc', which means 'fierce'.

Lucas is the Latin form of the Greek name Loukas, which means 'man from Lucania' – a district located in southern Italy.

Lucian was ultimately derived from Lucius, which originated from the Latin language and means 'light of the day'.

Luna originated from the Latin language and means 'of the moon'. In Roman mythology, Luna was the goddess of the moon.

Lux is a name that originated from the Latin language. It means 'filled with light', and was also used as a surname.

Lyle is an English name that was derived from the Old French words 'de' and 'isle', which mean 'from' and 'island'.

Lysander originated from the Old Greek name Lysandros. It was derived from 'lysis' and 'andros', which mean 'release' and 'man'.

M

Mabel is a variant of the Amabel, which was ultimately derived from the masculine name Amabilis – meaning 'adorable'.

Maddox was derived from the Welsh language and functions as a surname which means 'lucky one'.

Madonna originated from the Italian language and means 'lady of mine'. It is usually associated with images of the Virgin Mary.

Maggie originated as a pet form of Margaret. It was derived from the Hebrew word 'margaron' which means 'pearl'.

Magnus is said to have originated from the Latin language and means 'greatness'. It is mostly popular in the Scandinavian countries.

Mai is mostly associated with the Vietnamese language and means 'blossom of the apricot'.

Maisie was derived from the name Mairead, a version of Margaret which originated from the Greek language and means 'pearl'.

Maksim is a Russian verison of the name Maximus, which itself originated from the Latin word that means 'the greatest'.

Manolo was derived from the Greek 'Emmanouêl' and Hebrew 'immānūēl', which means 'God is with us'.

Marek is the Czech equivalent of Mark, which originated from the Latin language and is associated with the planet Mars.

Marina is commonly associated with water, as it was derived from the Latin word 'marinus' which means 'from the shore'.

Mark is the anglicised version of the Latin Marcus, which was inspired by the Roman god of war or the word 'mas' which means 'virile'.

Marley is actually an Old English surname derived from the name of a place that means 'from the lake meadow'.

Martel is said to have originated from the English language, but was derived from the French word 'martel' which means 'hammer'.

Mary was derived from Maria, which originated from the Hebrew name Miriam or Miryam. It could mean 'beloved' or 'rebelliousness'.

Mathilda was derived from the Germanic name Mathildis, which refers to 'power' or 'might in battle'.

Mattoe is the Italian version of Matthew. It originated from the Hebrew language and means 'God's present'.

Matthew is found in the Bible and originated from the Hebrew name Mattathyah, which means 'gift of Yahweh'.

Maureen is the anglicised version of Mairin, which was ultimately derived from the Biblical name Mary or Miryam in Hebrew – meaning 'rebellious'.

Maverick comes from the English word that was invented to mean 'non-conformist' or 'an independent and free spirit'.

Mavis originated from the Old French language and means 'song thrush'. It became popular in the 1930s.

Max was most probably derived from the Latin Maximus, which means 'greatest', and was used by aristocratic Roman families.

Maxine was derived from the name Maxima, which is the feminine form of Maximus. Similiar to Max, it means 'greatest'.

Maya most likely came from the Latin language and refers to the month of May.

Meda is most likely the shortened form of the names Almeda or Andromeda, which means 'achieving' or 'aware' respectively.

Mei means different things depending on how it is written in the Chinese language and most commonly refers to beauty.

Melina is said to be the dimunitive form of Melanie or Melissa, and was derived from the Greek word 'mel' which means 'honey'.

Melissa originated from the Greek word which means 'honey bee', and was borne by a nymph in Greek mythology.

Melody likely refers to the English word itself, which originated from the Greek language. It means 'song', 'music' or 'to sing'.

Mendel originated from the Hebrew language and was derived from the word 'minda' which means 'wisdom' or 'knowledge'.

Mia is considered to be another form of the name Mary, which originated from the Hebrew name meaning 'beloved' in Egypt.

Micah shares the same roots as Michael, which was derived from the Hebrew language and means 'which man is like God?'.

Miles was derived from the Germanic word 'milos' which means 'soldier'. In the Slavic language, 'mil' stands for 'favour' or 'grace'.

Mina originated from the Germanic language and means 'stout protector'. Mina also means 'coloured glass' in Persian.

Ming bears different meanings depending on how it is written in Chinese, but is commonly associated with enlightenment.

Miranda has its roots in the Latin language, and means 'wonderful' or 'she who deserves to be admired'.

Mirza originated from the Persian language, and refers to a noble man. In the olden days, it could only be borne by princes.

Molly is a variant of the name Mary, which is from the Bible. It was first used by the Irish, and most likely means 'rebellious'.

Morgan is the anglicised form of an old Welsh name Morcant, which was from the Celtic words 'mor' ('sea') and 'cant' ('circle').

Morris is a variant of Maurice, which was borrowed from the French and derived from the Latin word 'maurus' which means 'moor'.

N

Nadia is popular in the English-speaking world, but originated from the Russian name Nadezhda which means 'filled with hope'.

Naima is most likely the feminine form of the name Naim. In the Arabic language, it means 'calm'.

Naoki can bear different meanings, according to the way it is written in Japanese. Typically, it means 'honest tree' as a name.

Napoleon is associated with a powerful figure, but the name was typically given to people from the Italian city of Naples.

Nata has many possible origins. While it means 'hope' in Polish, it also refers to a speaker in Native American.

Natalie is the French form of Natalia in Latin which means 'Christmas day' and derived from the Latin word 'natalis' or 'birthday'.

Natasha is the diminutive of Natalya, which is the Russian form of the name Natalie. In French, the latter means 'Christmas day'.

Nathan came from the Hebrew name Nethan'el (or Nathaniel) which means 'God has given'.

Neil originated from the Gaelic language and could mean 'coming from clouds' or 'champion'.

Nero originated form the Latin language, but is most commonly found in the Italian-speaking world. It means 'the strong one'.

Nicholas is the anglicised spelling of the Greek name Nikolaos, which was originally derived from the words 'nike' ('victory') and 'laos' ('people'). The '-ch' spelling first appeared in the 12th century and became firmly embedded by the 16th century.

Nigel is a variant of Neil, and could have come from the Gaelic word which means 'champion', 'cloud' or 'passionate'.

Noah was derived from the Hebrew word 'noach' which means 'rest' or 'comfort', and is commonly associated with the Biblical ark.

Nolan was derived from the Irish name O'Nuallain. The word 'nuall' means 'famous' or 'champion'.

Nora is most likely the shortened form of Honora, which was ultimately derived from the Latin word meaning 'honour'.

Norman was derived from the Old Germanic words 'nord' which means 'north', and 'man' which literally translates to 'man'.

Octavio is the Spanish version of the name Octavius, which originated from the Latin language and refers to the eighth.

Oda was derived from Odessa in the western world, which means 'an odyssey' or 'long voyage' in Greek.

Oksana is the Russian version of the name Xenia, which originated from the Greek language. It means 'woman of hospitality'.

Oliver has many origins. Some say it refers to an elf warrior, but it is most commonly associated with peace and the olive branch.

Omar is mostly associated as the variant of Umar, which means 'flourishing' or 'prosperous' in the Arabic language.

Omega is meaningful due to the fact that it is the last letter in the Greek alphabet and is seen as a symbol of completion.

Orlando has been around since Medieval English times as Roland, which comes from the Germanic words that mean 'famous' and 'land'.

Oscar is a name that is said to have been derived from Irish mythology and is commonly associated with a 'friend of the deer'.

Otto was originally used as a pet name for any ancient Germanic name beginning with 'Od-' or 'Ot-' to mean 'wealth' or 'prosperity'.

Owen originated from the Latin name Eugenius, which was derived from the Greek word 'eugenes' and means 'well-born'.

P

Paco is actually a dimunitive of the name Franscisco, a Spanish/Portugese variant of the name Francis. In Latin, it refers to a French man.

Paloma is a popular name amongst Spanish-speaking families. It originated from the Latin language and means 'beautiful dove'.

Pandora is a name that is associated with the very first woman created by the gods in Greek mythology, and refers to gifts.

Parker was originally a surname that was derived from the old French word 'parchier', which means 'park-keeper'.

Pasqual is a Spanish version of Pascal, which originated from the Latin language and is commonly associated with Easter.

Patrick is a popular Irish name that actually comes from the Latin word 'patricius' which means 'nobly born'.

Patterson was a surname that was commonly used to refer to Patrick's son, but it originated in Latin and means 'nobleman'.

Paul was an old Roman family name which was derived from a nickname during the classical era, and means 'small' in Latin.

Pedro is the Portugese/Spanish version of the English name, Peter – which originated from Greek and means 'rock'.

Penelope originated from the Greek language and refers to a weaver. It could also have been a derivation of the expression 'duck'.

Peter is a name that was derived from the Greek word that refers to a stone or rock. It also has heavy Christian connotations.

Phoebe originated from the Greek name Phoibe, which was derived from the Greek word 'phoibos' which means 'bright'.

Philomena has its origins in the Greek language, and means 'strong love'. It was the name of a notable martyr in the Catholic church.

Phoenix is associated with the ancient, legendary bird in mythology all over the world – commonly related to resurrection.

Preston is an Old English name that is said to have been derived from the words that mean 'priest' and 'settlement' or 'town'.

Prudence was ultimately derived from the Latin word 'prudentia', which means 'wisdom, circumspection and practical judgment'.

Q

Quacy is believed to be a variant of the name Quacey, which alludes to moonlight in Scottish culture.

Queenie is usually used as an affectionate form of 'queen'. It could also be from the Old English word 'cwen' which means 'woman'.

Quentin is the Old French form of the Roman name Quintinus, which was derived from the Latin word 'quintus' that means the fifth.

Quiana is thought to be a variant of Hannah, which means 'favour' or 'grace'. It could also refer to a beautiful flower.

Quillan was derived from Hugelin, which contains the Germanic element 'hug' or 'heart, mind, and spirit'. In Latin, it refers to a sword.

Quinn is the anglicised form of the Gaelic name O'Cuinn, which means 'descendant of Conn'. The latter means 'chief' or 'leader'.

R

Rachel comes from the Hebrew word meaning 'ewe' and most likely grew popular due to the notable character in the Bible.

Rafael is a variant of Raphael, which is derived from the Hebrew words 'rafa' and 'el' – meaning 'to heal' and 'God' respectively.

Raoul is the French version of the Old Norse name Ralph. Ralph was derived from the words 'rad' and 'wulf' which mean 'advice' and 'wolf' respectively.

Raymond has Germanic roots, and comes from the elements 'ragin' which means 'advice', and 'mund' which means 'protector'.

Reagan was a popular surname in the Irish community and typically referred to Riagan's descendant.

Rebecca is a name that is said to have originated from the Bible and means 'bound' or 'captivating' in the Hebrew language.

Reese is a popular English name that actually originated from the Welsh language and means 'fervour' or 'enthusiasm'.

Reeta was derived from the name Margaret, which has Greek origins. Commonly found in Finnish communities, it means 'pearl'.

Reuben is a name that was derived from the Hebrew words 'raa' and 'ben', which mean 'to see' and 'my son' respectively.

Richard was derived from the nearly synonymous elements 'ric' which means 'powerful', and 'hard' meaning 'strong, hardy, and brave'.

Rihanna is a variation of Rhiannon, which was derived from the old Celtic name Rigantona which means 'great queen'.

Riley originated from the Old English language and is thought to be named after a place, meaning 'from a meadow of rye'.

Ringo is said to have originated from the Japanese word that refers to an apple. It was popularised by The Beatles' drummer.

Ronald was derived from the Old Norse elements 'regin' which means 'advice' or 'decision', and 'valdr' which means 'ruler'.

Rosa originated from the Latin language as a variant form of Rose. Rose most likely refers to the fragrant flower itself.

Roy is the anglicised version of the Scottish-Gaelic Ruadh which means 'red'. It could also be from the French word 'roi' or 'king'.

Ruby was derived from the gemstone of the same name. It could also have originated from the Latin word 'rubeus' or 'red'.

Ryan originated from the Irish surname O'Riain, which is made out of the elements 'Rí' or 'king' and the suffix '-an' – forming 'little king'.

S

Sadie was derived from Sarah, the English name with Biblical connections. It means 'princess' or 'ladylike' in the Hebrew language.

Sally is a diminutive form of the name Sarah, which means 'little princess'. It is one of the oldest female given names on record.

Samantha was most likely inspired by the name Samuel, combined with the feminine suffix '-antha' which means 'flower' in Greek.

Samara originated from the Hebrew language and means 'watched over by God'. It also has Arabic roots, and means 'night talking'.

Savannah is a fairly modern name that refers to the English word that refers to a 'grassland without trees'.

Sawyer was derived from the Old English words 'sagu' or 'saghe' which means 'a person who saws wood'.

Scarlett is a variation of the word and name Scarlet – derived from the Old French word 'escarlate' for top-quality fabric or rich cloth.

Sebastian was derived from the Latin Sebastianus, a name for people who came from Sebastos in Greece, and means 'revered'.

Serena originated from Latin, and means 'incredibly calm'. It was famously borne by a saint in the western Roman empire.

Silas was derived from the name Silvanus, which comes from the Latin word 'silva' that means 'wood'.

Simon is the English form of the Hebrew name Simeon which means 'hearkening'. It has been popular for centuries.

Skylar originated from the Dutch language, as a derivative of the name Schuyler. It is thought to mean 'scholar'.

Sophia comes from the Greek word 'sophos' which means 'wisdom'. In medieval times, it grew popular because of Sophia the Martyr.

Stella came from the Latin word 'stella', which is rooted in the Indo-European word that means 'star'.

Steven originated from the Greek language and refers to a 'man with crown'. Saint Stephen is thought to be the first Christian martyr.

Sydney is commonly associated with the Australian city, but actually originated from Old English and means 'from a large island'.

T

Taylor is an English surname that was derived from the occupational word 'tailleor' in Anglo-Norman, which means 'cutter'.

Terence is a popular English name that was actually derived from the Latin name Terentius, which possibly means 'soft' or 'tender'.

Theodore originated from the Greek language and although it is spelt differently all over the world, it means 'God's present'.

Thomas is the English form of the Greek word 'didymus' which was derived from the Aramaic word 'ta'oma' which means 'the twin'.

Tiffany was derived from Theophania, which means 'epiphany'. It comes from the Greek elements meaning 'God' and 'to appear'.

Timothy was derived from the Greek name Timotheos, which contains the elements of 'time' ('honour') and 'theos' ('God').

Titania most probably came from the Latin word 'titanius' which means 'of the Titans'.

Toby is the shortened form of Tobias, which is the Greek version of the Hebrew name Tobiah which means 'Yahweh is good'.

Tony is said to be the abbreviation of Anthony and has been around since medieval times. Like the name Anthony, it means 'praiseworthy'.

Travis was originally used as a surname that was derived from the occupation relating to a 'traverser', which means 'to cross'.

Tristan was the older version of the name Drustan. The latter came into being from Celtic mythology, and embodies boldness.

Tyler originated from the occupation of tile-making. In Old English, the word 'tigele' referred to tiles, bricks, and roofing shingle.

U

Ulrich was derived from the Germanic words 'uodal' and 'ric', which mean 'heritage' or 'inheritance' and 'rich' or 'powerful' respectively.

Umut is a name with Turkish origins and typically means 'full of hope'.

Una is the anglicised form of the feminine Latin word 'unus'. It symbolises truth, unity, and the one true church.

Ursula is the diminutive form of the Latin word 'ursa' which means 'she-bear'. It is also used in the names of celestial constellations.

Usha is a name of Hindi and Sanskrit origins, and means 'dawn'. In Hindu mythology, it is borne by the daughter of heaven.

Uta literally means 'song' in Japanese, and could be the shortened form of the German Otthild which means 'prospers in battle'.

V

Valentina is popular in Europe, but it originated from the Latin language and is thought to mean 'strong' and 'sound'.

Vanessa could have been derived from 'phanessa', an ancient Greek word for a mystic divinity.

Veda originated from Sanskrit, and means 'wisdom and knowledge'. In the Hindu culture, the Vedas are the four sacred books.

Veronica is the Latin form of the Greek name Berenice which was derived from elements 'pherein' ('to bring') and 'nike' ('victory').

Victor originated from the Latin word meaning 'conqueror' and has been in use since the ancient Roman times.

Violet originated from the Old French word 'violette' or 'viola' in Latin, and refers to a certain kind of bluish-purple flower.

Viva is a unique name that most probably originated from the Latin word 'aviva' which means 'alive'.

Vivian originated from the Latin language, and means 'full of life'. It was famously borne by a Roman martyr and French saint.

W

Walden is an English name that refers to a 'child of the forest valley'.

Wanda has Germanic roots and typically refers to people from the Vandal tribe. The Vandals were of Slavic origins.

Wesley came from the words 'wes' which signifies the western direction, and 'leah' which means a 'wood clearing' or 'meadow'.

Whitney is said to have originated from the Old English phrase 'atten whiten ey' which means 'by the white island'.

William originated from the Germanic words 'wil' which means 'will' or 'desire', and 'helm' which means 'helmet' or 'protection'.

Willow originated from the Old English language, and is taken from the willow tree – also known as the queen of waters.

Wright probably started off as an occupation and means 'carpenter'. As a given name, it has been around since the 19th century.

Wyatt has Anglo-Saxon origins and was derived from the English name Wigheard, which means 'war' and 'brave' or 'hardy'.

X

Xanthe is a name that may not be all that common, but it is thought to have originated from the Greek language and means 'golden'.

Xavier started off as a medieval surname which was derived from a place, the Basque Etxeberri, which means 'the new house'.

Xenia originated from the Greek word 'hospitality', and is a derivative form of the word 'xenos' which means 'foreigner' or 'guest'.

Xiu differs in meaning depending on how it is written in the Chinese language, but it typically refers to someone charming.

Xuxa is the Latin version of the English name, Susan, which originated from the Hebrew language and refers to the lily flower.

Xylander is said to have come from the Greek words 'xylon' which means 'wood' or 'forest', and 'andros' which means 'man'.

Y

Yaron is a traditional name that is the equivalent of the English Jaron which means 'full of joy', 'to shout', or 'to sing'.

Yasmin was ultimately derived from the Old Persian word 'yasamen' which refers to the jasmine flower.

Yasuhiro differs in meaning depending on how it is written in Japanese. Typically, it means 'abundant honesty' or 'widespread peace'.

Yogi traditionally refers to a practitioner of yoga and originated from India. It has gained popularity in recent years.

Yoko is a common name in Japan, like most Japanese names with the traditional '-ko' ending. It means 'sunshine child'.

Yolanda was derived from the name Violet, which originated in the Latin language and refers to the popular purple flower.

Yuki is a word that could mean 'snow' or 'happiness' in Japanese. As a name, it could refer to bravery and gentle hope.

Yvette is the feminine equivalent of the French Yves, which contains the Germanic element 'iwa' which means 'yew'.

Z

Zack is the shortened version of Zachary or Zachariah, which originated from the Hebrew words that mean 'to remember' and 'God'.

Zahra or **Zara** has its origins in the Arabic language and means 'radiant'.

Zareh is an Armenian name that is said to mean 'tears' or 'protector', and was borne by a legendary king in the History of Armenia.

Zeb is the shortened version of the name Zebediah, which originated from the Hebrew language and means 'God lends'.

Zelda is thought to be from an Old English word which means 'companion'. Other sources say that it means 'a dark battle' in German.

Zendaya is said to have originated from the word for 'thanks' in the Shona language, which is spoken in Zimbabwe.

Zetta likely originated from the Latin word that refers to the number 7, due to its association with luck and how modern it sounds.

Zita either originated from the Italian word which means 'young girl', or the Greek word which means 'seeker'.

Zoë originated from the Greek word that means 'life'. It has been in use since the Roman times and continues to be popular.

Lio Yeung is an art director and visual artist based in
Hong Kong. As a recipient of the 2009 Hong Kong Young
Design Award and a seasoned creative professional in the
advertising industry, his work has been recognised locally
and internationally at Cannes, D & AD, The One Show, and
the Clio Awards, among others. Besides founding the Young
and Innocent creative collective and Art Glossary magazine,
he has held solo exhibitions and published his first book
called 'IF Red is Green'.

Illustrations and text © 2018 Lio Yeung
Designed and edited by Viction Workshop Ltd.

Published by

VICTI●N
VICTI●N

www.victionary.com

Viction Workshop Ltd.
7C Seabright Plaza, 9–23 Shell Street, North Point, Hong Kong
 victionviction   victionviction

©2018 viction:workshop ltd.
All rights reserved. No part of this book may be reproduced,
transmitted, or stored anywhere by any means, graphic,
electronic or mechanical without prior written permission
from the publisher.

Publisher's note: All name meanings, origins, and
pronunciations were aggregated from various online
and offline data currently available.

FIRST EDITION 2018

ISBN 978-988-77747-5-4
Printed in China

3 1333 04713 4976